A Gallery of KNOTS!

A Beginner's How-to Guide

By Tara Cousins
ISBN: 9781711344492
Copyright © 2014 Tara Cousins
Tiger Road Publishing
www.TigerRoadCrafts.com

Introduction

Welcome to **A Gallery of KNOTS!** Knot tying is a very versatile craft, accessible to everyone with hands and some string. With the wide range of materials, there are many projects for you to make, ranging from easy key chains to more complex belts and jewelry. This book will teach you some basic knots by using step-by-step photos and descriptions to guide you on your way. The book starts out with basic knots and moves on to some more complex designs. **Often, previous knots are referred back to, so it is best to read the book in order; however, feel free to skip around a bit if something specifically catches your fancy!**

A note about terminology: Since the art of knot tying spans a wide range of crafting genres, certain vocabulary may be different than what you have heard elsewhere or seen written on the internet. I have done my best to be as accurate as possible when using terminology, based on the art of macramé, needlecrafts, and paracord crafts. Don't forget to read through the "Getting Started" section. It explains some of the terminology this book uses and it gives you some guidance about how to start and finish your projects.

Tying knots may seem simple at first, but some of the designs require a little patience and extra practice to get just right. Most of all have fun and enjoy!

How to Make Stuff with Your Knots

Once you have learned and practiced your knot tying skills, you will certainly want to make stuff!

Materials

Most materials are quite affordable, so play around with different items to find the look and feel that you like best. Remember, when working with different materials, you may have to adjust how tightly you pull your knots. For example, nylon cording can be pulled nice and tight and still tends to loosen up over time, whereas if you pull stretchy wool yarn too tightly your whole project may not turn out right at all.

As you can see in the photo, there is a wide range of fibers for you to use. Most of the how-to photos in this book use paracord because it shows off the knots well and the knotted designs are very easy to see. Paracord comes in different thicknesses and can be bought at most hardware stores and even big box stores in the craft section. You can also use thinner nylon cord for smaller projects. For jewelry, I recommend using hemp cord, which comes in various colors and thicknesses. You will see hemp cord used in many of the jewelry examples in this book. Embroidery floss, which is commonly used to make friendship bracelets, is also a good option for jewelry. I have used cotton clothesline, wool or acrylic yarn, jute twine, and plain cotton string for different projects as well.

You may also want and need some additional items to embellish your project and to help in making it. **Scissors**, of course, are a necessity. If working with paracord or nylon cord, you will also want a basic **lighter**. When the ends of the cord are held under the flame for a few seconds, the cord melts slightly and the ends are "cured" so that they don't unravel. Just be careful not to burn yourself! (Grownups be sure to help your kids do this and don't let the young ones use the lighter - the burnt ends get extremely hot). You will also need to figure out how to secure your project while you work on it so that it doesn't move around. I like to use a basic **clipboard** but you can also use **tape** to hold down your strands or a **safety pin**, or anything else you can think of to hold the ends in place while you tie the knots (when I was a kid, I held onto the ends between my toes!).

Clasps

First you will need to decide what type of project you would like to make. Jewelry projects require a basic clasp. To do this you will need some sort of loop in one end and some sort of knob in the other end to stick in the loop. Look in the photo at left and you will see an assortment of clasps. In the top paracord bracelet example, a large washer is used. You can use a large bead instead for the same sort of closure. In the next bracelet, a commercially bought toggle connector jewelry clasp is used. You can also use a fancy plastic clasp like the black one in the photo. If you are making a keychain, simply work your project directly onto a key ring. Or, use a carabiner or fancy dog leash attachment.

Mounting Knots

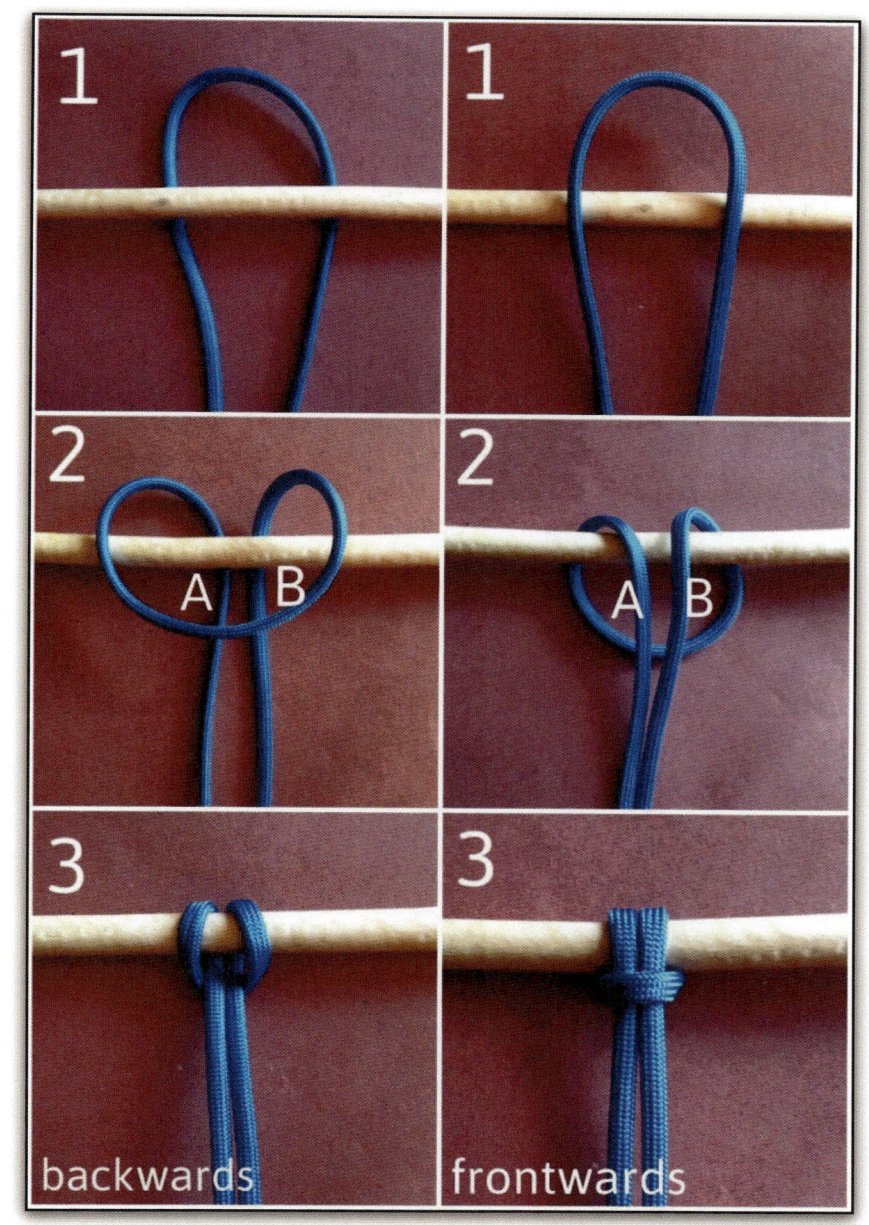

Once you decide on your clasp, you will need to attach your strands so that you can start your knot tying.

There are a few different ways to begin working. If you are working with multiple strands you can simply tie a knot to secure the ends together (see *overhand* knot in next section). Or, if you are using a clasp such as a key ring, carabiner, etc. then you can attach your strands directly to the object. To do this without having any cut ends, fold your strands in half and use the mounting knot. This type of knot, otherwise known as a **Lark's Head**, can be attached either frontwards or backwards.

To attach backwards, start with the loop in back, fold it over, and pull strands A and B through to the front.

To attach frontwards, start with the loop in front, fold it over the back, and pull both A and B strands through to the back.

Butterflies

If you are working with very long strands and you don't want them to tangle up while you work, you can make a **butterfly** for each strand. To do this, fold up the strand in a figure eight pattern (photo 1) and secure with a rubber band around the center (photo 2). By doing this, you can easily pull out the strand as you need it.

Helpful hint: Start with longer lengths of strands than you think you might need. It is always best to have to trim off extra length instead of realizing too late that you are going to come up short! Wasting a little material is almost always better than having to undo your knots or start a project over from the beginning.

Sinnets

The word **sinnet** (sometimes spelled **sinnit**) is used to mean a length of knots with a repeating pattern. Traditionally, sinnets are used to neatly store long length of rope for later storage. There are many ways to form sinnets so that they unravel easily. In macramé and jewelry making, the knots may not be able to easily come undone for later use, but the word sinnet is still used.

Foundation Strands and Working Strands

The **foundation strands** are lengths of string that are hidden inside your project and do not "move" as you work. They run the vertical length and form the backbone of the fancy knots. They can also be referred to as "drones" or "filler cords."

The other strands, the ones you work/tie with, are often called the **working strands.** You will see that some of the more advanced knots have multiple working strands and multiple foundation strands. The foundation strands only need to be slightly longer than your desired finished length, whereas the working strands need to be two, three, or more times longer.

The Knot Gallery

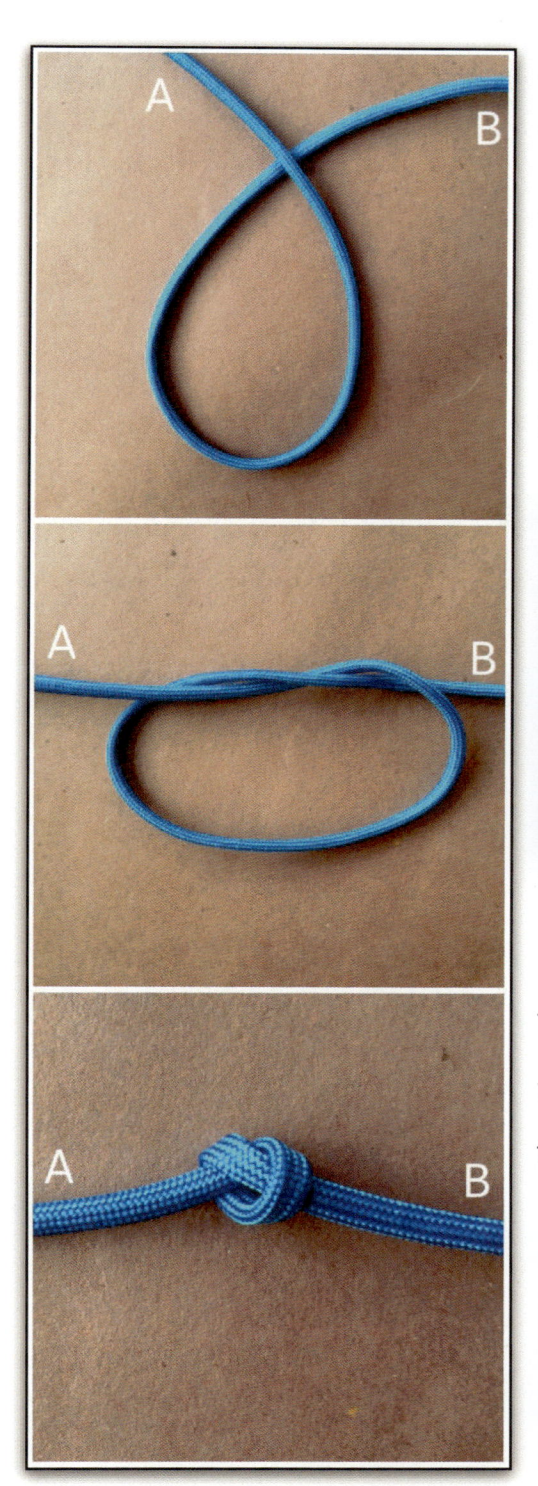

Overhand Knot

This is a very basic knot, that pretty much everyone knows and uses (the first step to tying your shoes). It is commonly used as a way to start or finish off a project.

The basic overhand knot can be used to secure a group of strands at the beginning or end of a project, as seen in the photo below.

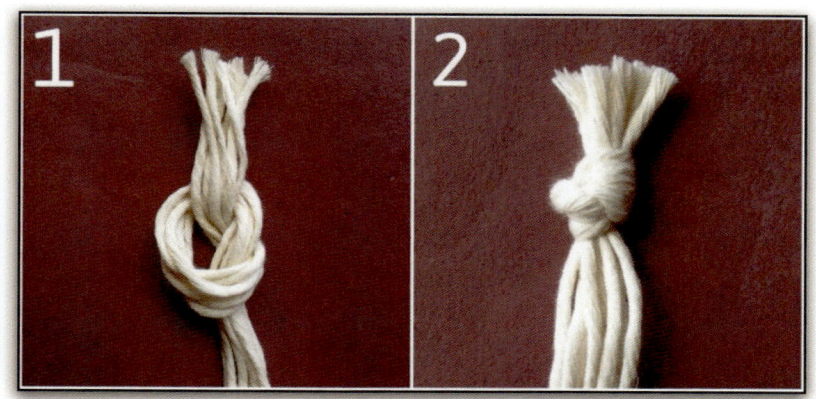

Barrel Knot

To make this knot, begin to form an overhand knot but wind the A strand around several times before pulling tight. This knot can also be called a *wrap* or *coil* knot.

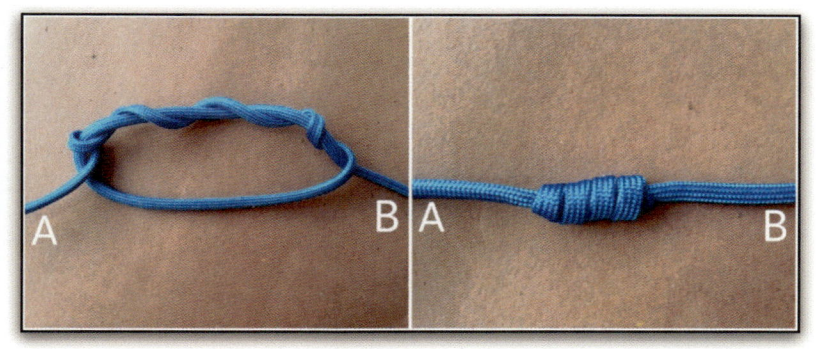

Gathering Knot

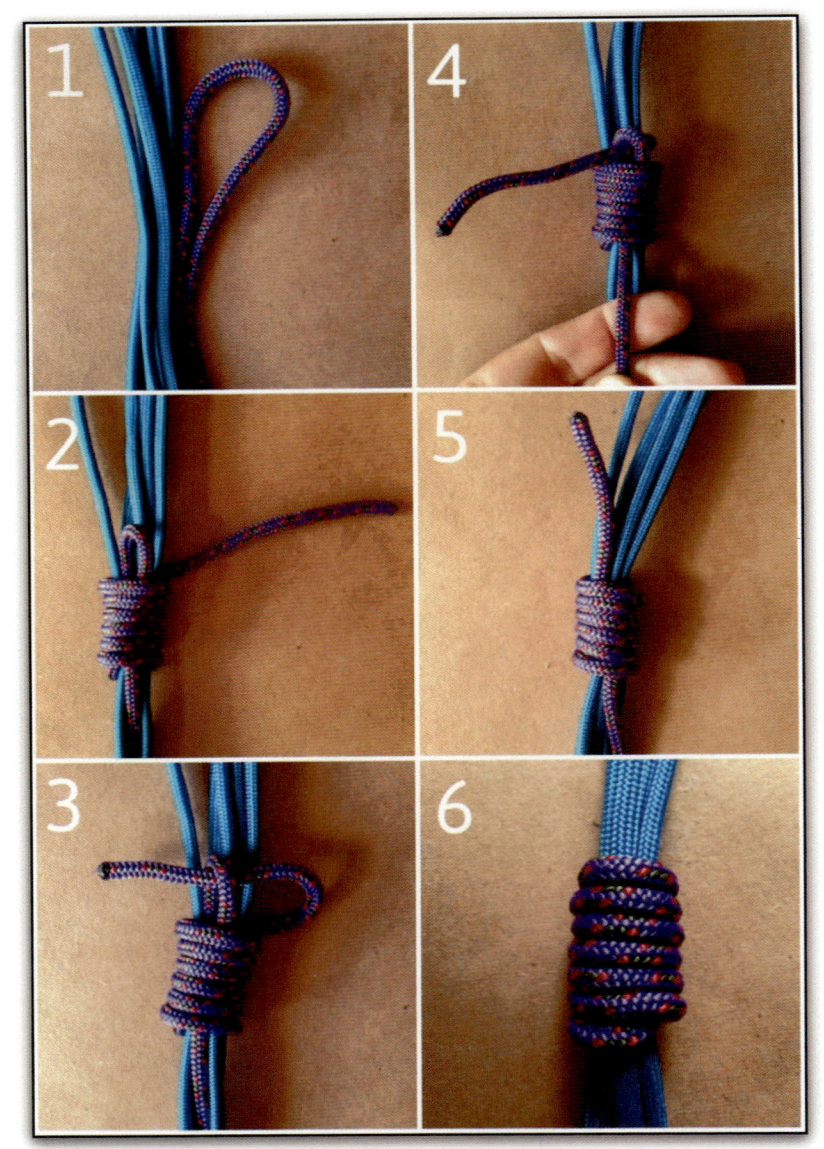

This knot can be used to bind together a group of cords or strands, and has a neat finished appearance. First, start with a loop in one end of the gathering cord you would like to use. Place the loop up against the filler cords (photo 1). Hold the base of the cord secure with one hand and with the other, wrap the gathering cord around all strands, starting at the bottom and working over the loop. Keep the top of the loop exposed (photo 2). Next, place the end of the gathering cord through the loop (photo 3). Pull down on the bottom of the gathering cord (photo 4) so that the looped end is pulled inside and hidden (photo 5). You can then trim the ends of the gathering cord so they are completely hidden inside (photo 6).

8

Half Hitches

There are two ways to work a half hitch: labeled in the photos as #1 and #2. As I work them, I like to call them either the "over-under" or "under-over" so I don't get confused.

The first half hitch, #1, is the over-under type. See photos below. Notice how strand B stays still, and strand A goes over and under B.

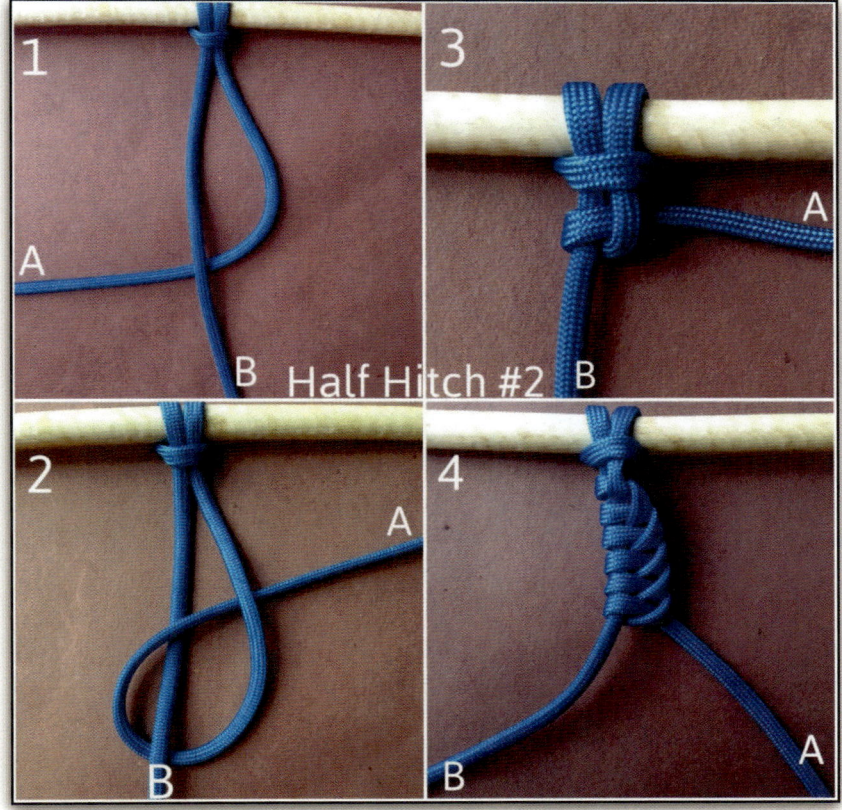

The next half hitch, #2, is the under-over type. See photos below. Notice how strand B stays still, and strand A goes under and over B. When working a project all in this half hitch knot, you will need to start out with a very long strand A and a strand B only as long as you would like the finished project to be.

9

Project: Simple Friendship bracelet

To make this bracelet, you will need :

- 3 strands of embroidery floss, cut approx. 6ft long. They will be folded in half for a total of 6 strands (lengths may vary depending on the size of the bracelet and how often the colors are switched)

- A jewelry clasp. A toggle connector works best, as seen in the photo.

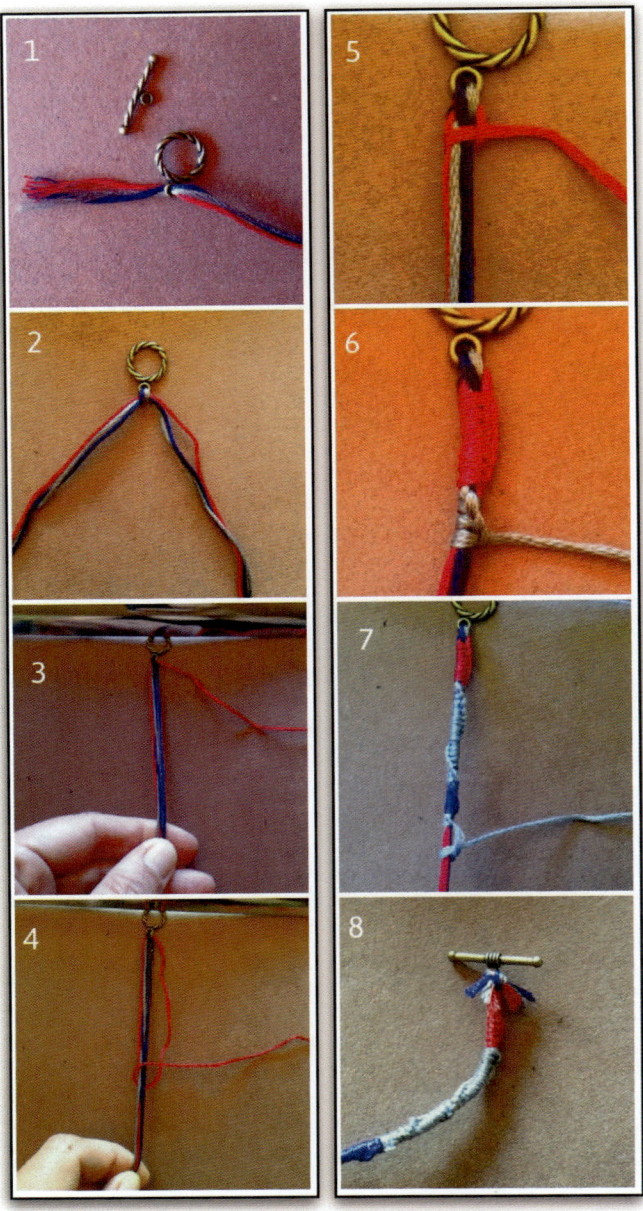

To begin, thread the strands through one end of the clasp (photo 1), and tie an overhand knot in the very middle of the strands (photo 2). To make it easier, wet and twist the strands to get them all through. Secure to a clipboard and pick a strand in the first color you would like to use (photo 3). With this strand, work a Half Hitch #2 (the under-over type) around the rest of the strands (photos 4 and 5). Continue working half hitches in this manner, tightening them gently as you work. The knots will begin to naturally form a spiral. When you would like to switch colors, simply pull out another strand and work the same type of half hitch with it, around all the other strands (photos 6 and 7). Once you have reached your desired length, thread the other side of the clasp through the strands and tie an overhand knot securely, and trim your ends (photo 8).

Project: Half Hitch Spiral Dog Leash

This fancy dog leash uses only the basic knots you have learned so far.

To make this leash, you will need :

- At least 30 ft of cord or rope (this will make a leash approx. 5 ft long, more cord can be used for a longer leash).

- Some sort of clasp - a carabiner or a clip as in the photo

First, fold your cord so that there is about 6 ft on one side, 24 ft on the other. Make a barrel knot near the fold. Thread your clasp through and make a second barrel knot on the other side of the clasp (photo 1). Fold your leash and make and overhand knot just below the barrel knots (photo 2). Next, secure your project to a clipboard. You may choose to use a butterfly because the working strand will be very long.

With the working strand, work a sinnet of Half Hitches #2 for about 6" (photo 4). Then, add a little fancy detailed section. Make 3 overhand knots on each strand, work an overhand knot while holding both strands together, then make 3 more overhand knots on each strand (this section shown in photo 5). Continue repeating a pattern of 6" of half hitches, then the fancy

11

detailed section as many times as you would like. Near the end, make a long 12" section of half hitches for the handle. Fold the handle over and secure to the base of the leash with a couple of overhand knots.

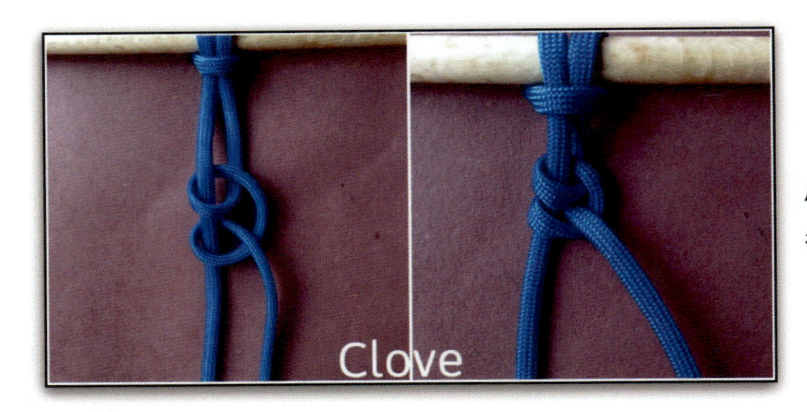

Clove Hitch

A Clove hitch is formed by working two #1 half hitches (over-unders).

Lark's Head

A Lark's Head is formed by working a half hitch #1 and then a half hitch #2. Notice how it looks a lot like a mounting knot.

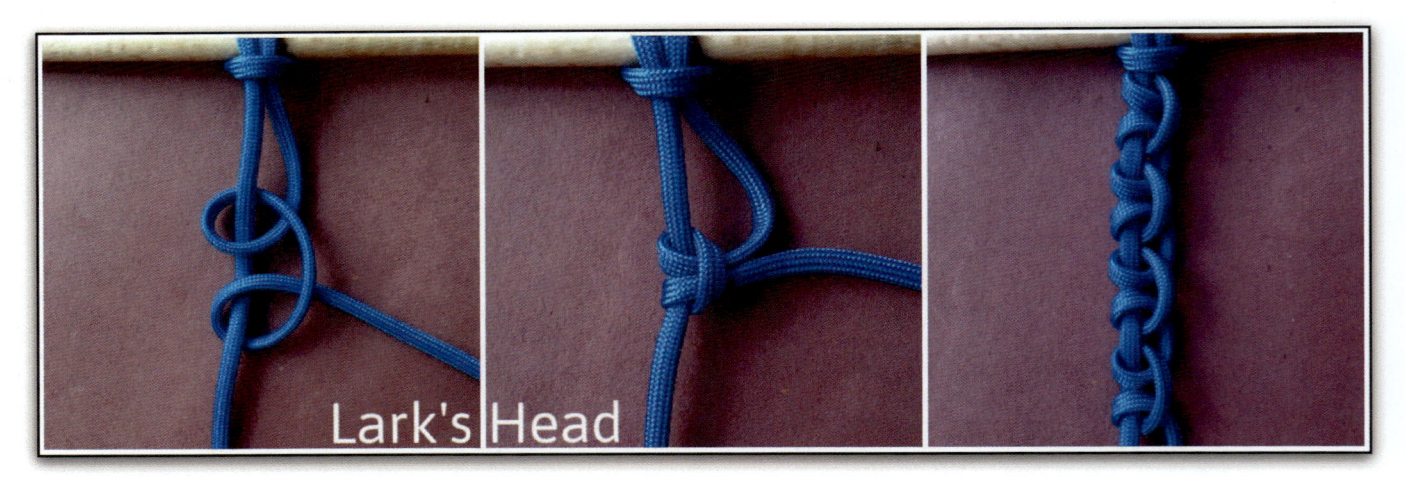

You can also work these knots in the opposite direction. Notice how in the above examples, the left hand strand was held still, and the right hand strand was worked around it. Let's say you decide to instead keep the **right** strand still, and work the **left** one around it. In this manner you can make an "opposite" or "left hand" knot. The two projects that come next will show you how to work regular as well as lefty knots.

Project: Alternating Lark's Head Keychain

The materials for this project will vary according to what you would like to make. The pictured item was made with two 4-foot strands of hemp cord, folded in half.

To make this chain, mount 2 strands to a clasp (photo 1: this makes 4 strands to work with). The two outside strands will be the working strands. The two center strands stay still – they are the foundation strands. The inside two strands only need to be slightly longer than your desired finished length and the two outside strands need to be about twice as long.

To begin, start with the strand on the far right and tie a Lark's head around the middle two (photos 2, 3, and 4).

Next, use the strand on the far left to tie a "lefty" Lark's head around the middle two. For

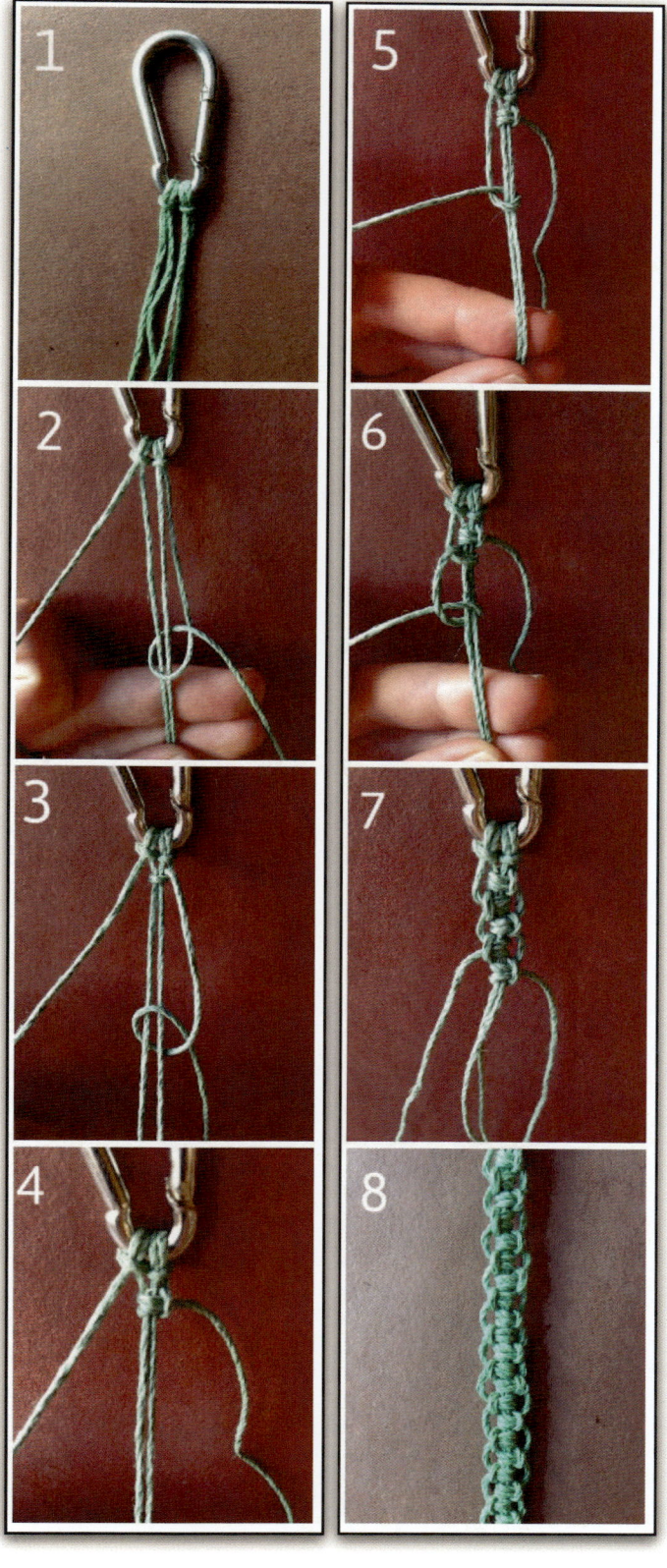

13

the left side, it helps to hold the middle strands in your right hand and the left strand in your left hand. Remember, do the over-under then the under-over, as shown is photos 5 and 6. The knots are basically the same but since you are working on the left, you will pull and tighten out to the left.

Continue alternating the lark's head, using the outside right strand and then the outside left strand (photo 7). A pretty chain will form, as shown in photo 8.

Project: Lark's Head Double Chain

This lacy mesh provides a nice flat and wide project. It would make a pretty choker necklace, belt, or keychain, depending on the materials used. The example was worked with hemp cord.

You will need 3 strands, folded in half and mounted on a clasp, for a total of 6 strands.

The strands are numbered in the first photo. Strands #2 and #5 do not work or move.

Step 1: Using strand #1, tie a lefty lark's head over strand #2 (photo 2) and using strand #6, tie a righty lark's head over strand #5 (photo 3)

Step 2: Using strand #3, tie a righty lark's head over strand #2 (photo 4) and using strand #4, tie a lefty lark's head over strand #5 (shown in photo 5)

Step 3: (same as step 1) #1 does left lark's over #2, #6 does right lark's over #5 (end of step 3 shown in photo 5)

Step 4: using strand #4, tie a righty lark's head over strand #2 and using strand #3, tie a lefty lark's head over strand #5 (end of step 4 shown in photo 6).

Now, repeat steps 1 through 4 until you reach your desired length.

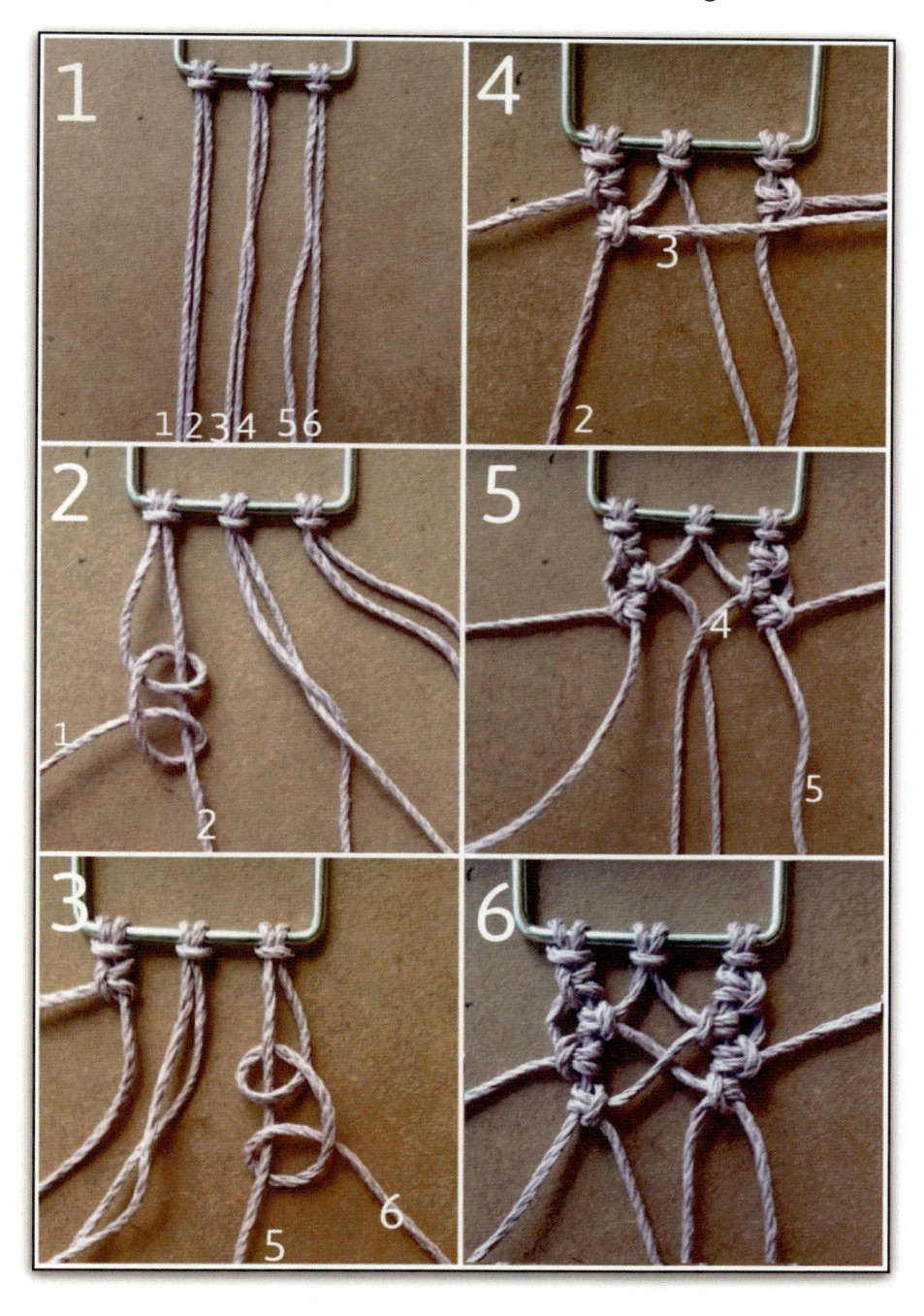

15

Half Knot

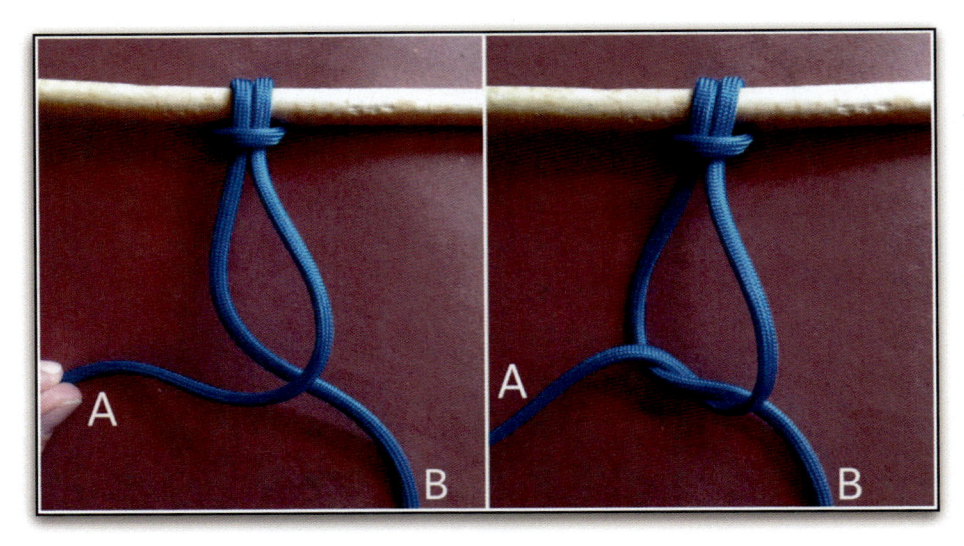

To make a half knot, cross strand A (the strand starting on the right) over B, then pull A up through.

Square Knot

A square knot is formed by first making a half knot, and then making another half knot in the opposite direction, as shown in the photos. Continuing from the half knot, take the same A strand (now on the left), cross over and up through. Pull to tighten.

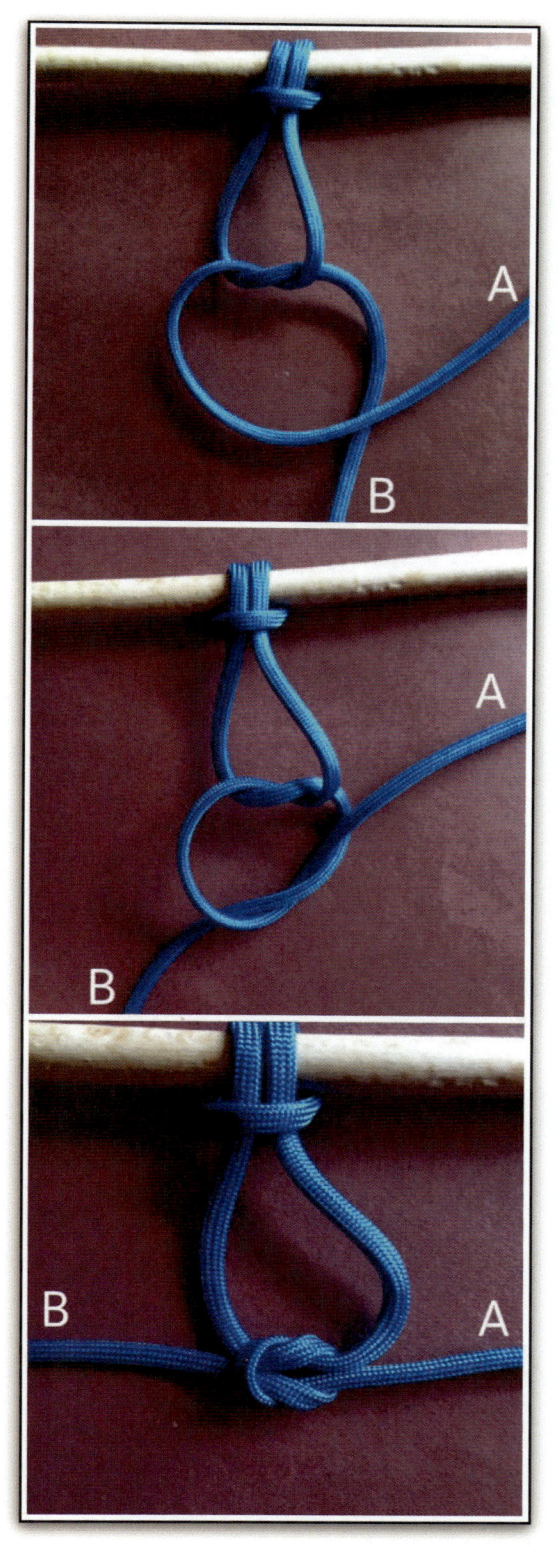

If you keep making square knots, a pretty pattern emerges. However, you will notice this length is not very thick and strong. In order to make a project that won't stretch out of shape and that will be strong enough, you need to use center foundation strands. I will show you how to do this on the next page, with the Paracord Cobra Project.

17

Project: Paracord Cobra

The basic paracord bracelet is a sinnet of square knots worked around foundation strands. The photo shows the foundation strands in orange, and the working blue strands will be worked around them. The orange strands will not move and they only need to be slightly longer than your desired finished length. The blue outside strands need to be approx. 3 times as long as your desired length.

For the example, I mounted two strands, folded in half, over a wood dowel. If you are making a bracelet, use one of the clasp types as show in the "how to make stuff" section.

To make the cobra weave, you will tie square knots over the center two strands. I have labeled the working strands A and B (photo 1). Take strand A and cross it under B. Notice how the strands look like the number "4" (photo 2). Take B and fold it up and through (photo 3). Pull tight (photo 4).

Now, take A and cross it under B forming an opposite number "4" shape (photo 5). Fold B up and through (photo 6). Pull tight (photo 7). Continue alternating sides, making regular "4" shapes and opposite "4" shapes. A pretty pattern will emerge (photo 8).

To finish off your bracelet, you can thread a washer, large bead, etc. through all strands and tie in an overhand knot. This end can be inserted into the beginning loop. Or, you can use a pre-made bracelet clasp, similar to the examples shown in the previous section. Remember, once you cut your paracord ends, use a lighter to seal them up so they don't unravel. You can also melt ends together.

19

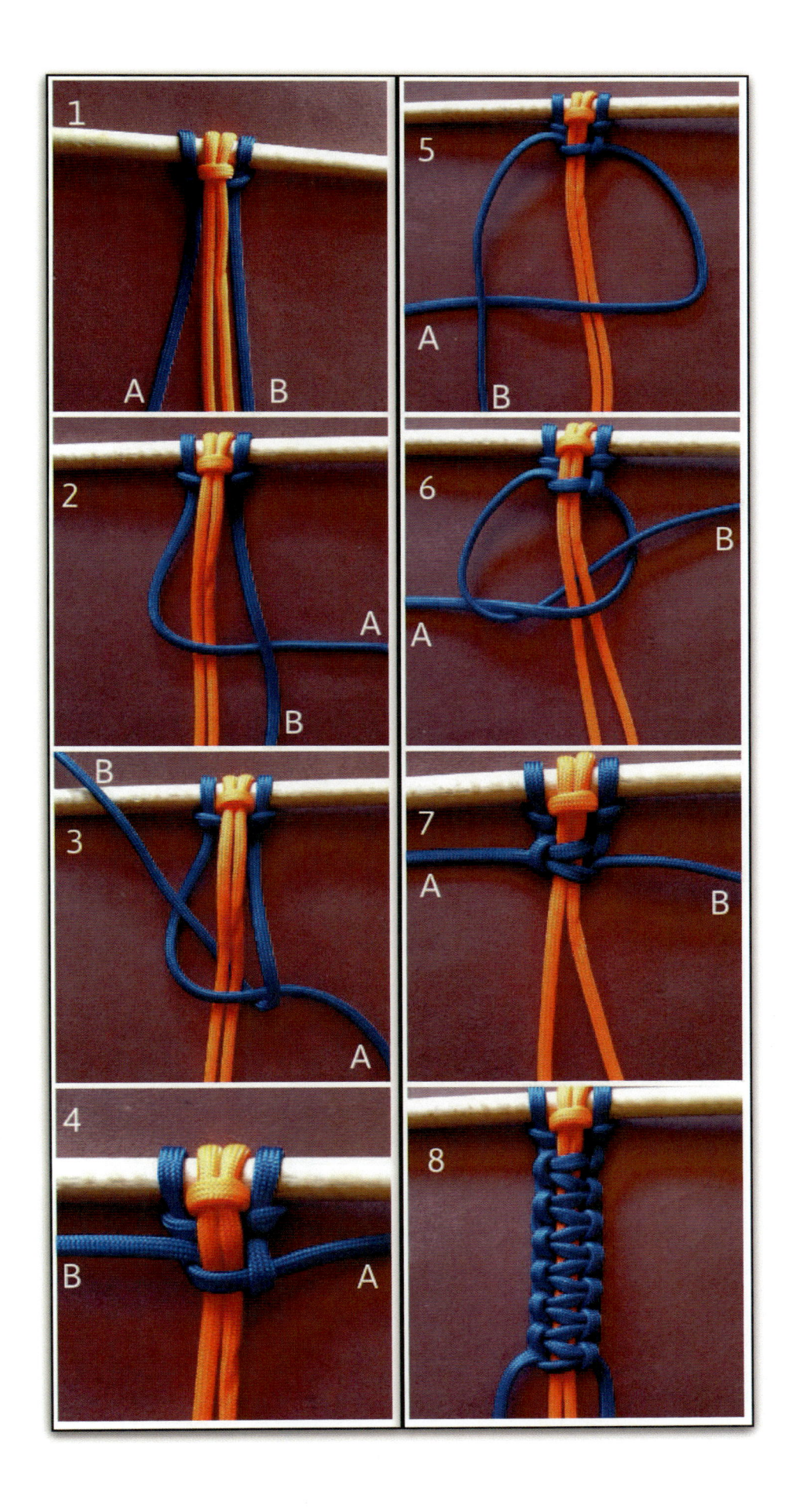

Project: Half Knot Sinnet Keychain Worked with Double Strands

This project only uses half knots so it seems a bit easier than the cobra paracord bracelet, however, you will be working with double strands so it takes a little bit of practice to keep all of them straight! For the example, I chose to use a soft white cotton string. You will need 3 lengths, folded in half.

To begin, line up all three strands together and use a single mounting knot to attach to a key ring (photo 1). Separate the strands into three groups of two (photo 2). The two center strands are the foundation strands and will not move. As in the previous project, make the number "4" (photo 3). Bring the right hand strand up and through (photo 4). Pull to tighten, keeping the working strands pulled straight down (photo 5).

Repeat these steps and the work will start to form a spiral. As the work spirals around (photo 7), you might get confused as to which strands are which. To keep them organized, you can use a marker to color the bottoms. Also, if you find they are unraveling, use a little tape on the ends (photo 8).

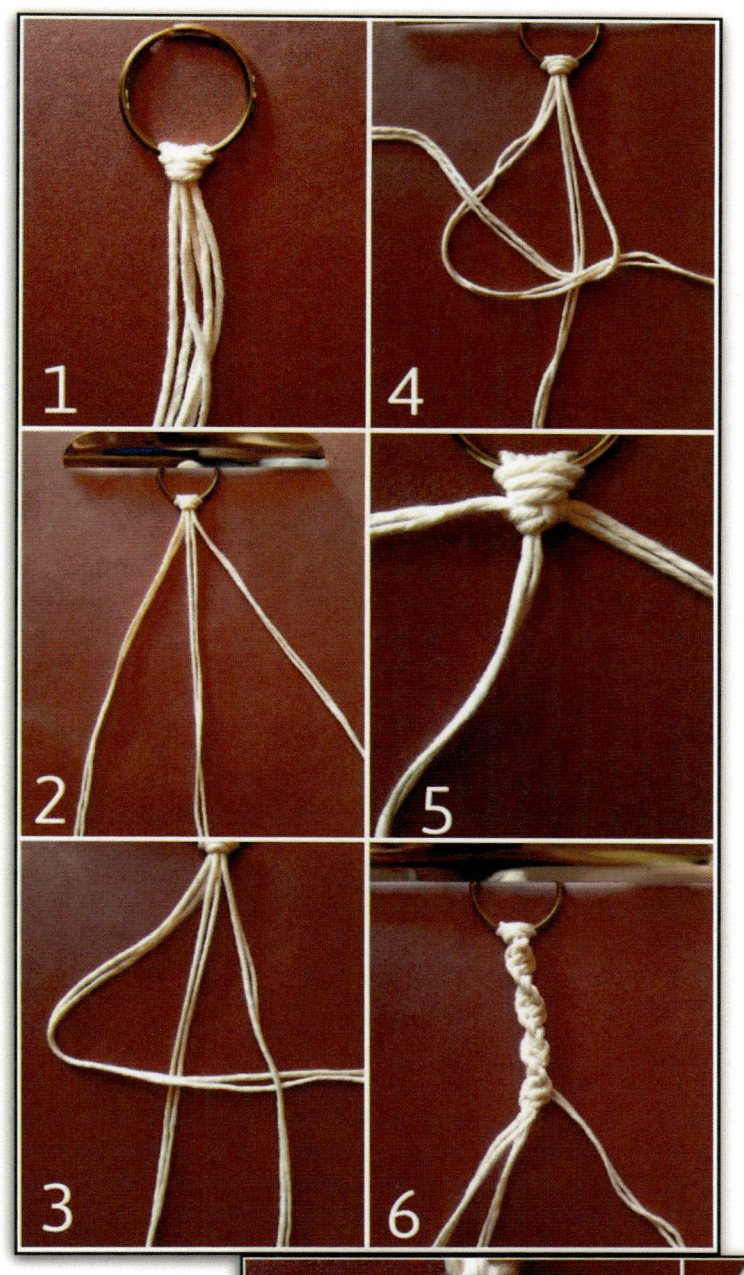

Once your keychain is the desired length, you can add decorative beads (taping your ends will also help with threading through beads). Lastly, tie an overhand knot with all strands to secure them

Project: Loops/Picots and Beads Keychain

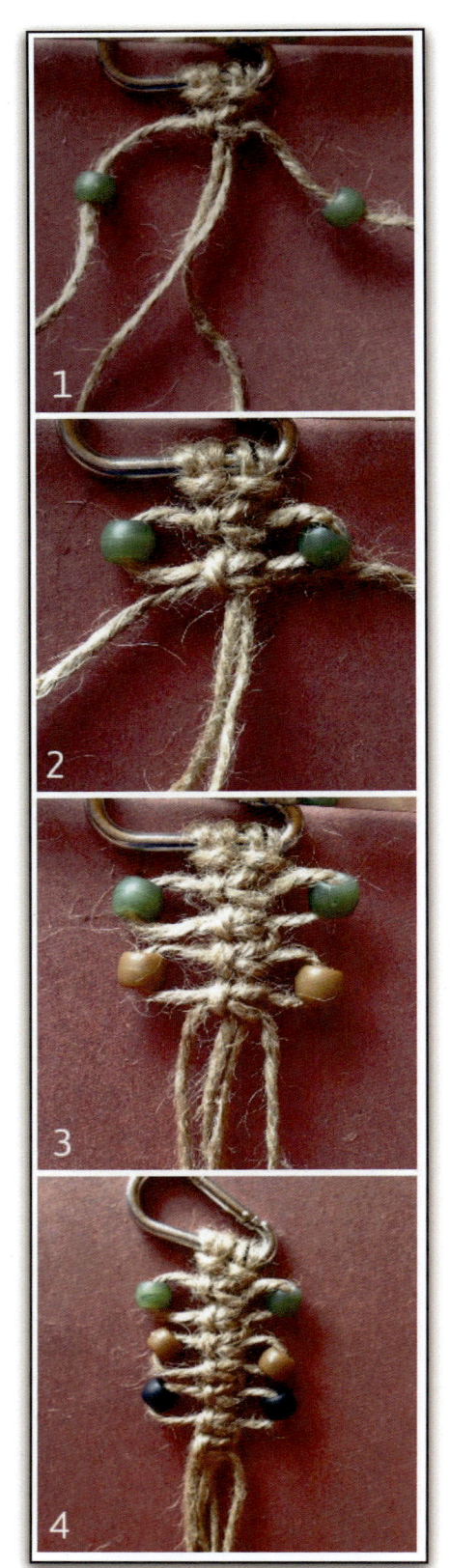

This project will show you how to make loops in your sinnet chain. Often in crafting, loops are called "picots." If you like, you can easily add beads to your picots. The example project was made with 2 four foot lengths of jute twine, folded and mounted on a carabiner.

The directions assume you have read over (and hopefully tried to work through!) the previous example projects, and are now familiar with making square knots over foundation strands.

To make this keychain, you will need 4 total strands - 2 outside working strands and 2 inside foundation strands. *Make a regular square knot, then thread two beads, one on each working strand (photo 1). Next make another square knot, keeping strands loose where the beads are. Push up and tighten, leaving the bead strands loose (photo 2).* Repeat the directions from * to * for desired length. Notice how you can easily adjust the size of the loops, longer or shorter (photos 2 and 3). When you have made a sinnet to your desired length, tie a basic overhand knot to secure the ends and trim.

Alternating Square Knot Pattern

This is such a pretty pattern that can make a very wide flat fabric. Depending on the materials you use, this could make a very pretty belt. The example was worked with a wool/acrylic blend medium weight yarn. Yarn can be difficult to work with because it stretches quite a bit, but the finished product is soft and cozy. You can use as many strands as you like, as long as they are in a multiple of 4. I would recommend using at least 16 (8 folded in half) as in the example.

This project assumes you are familiar with making square knots as shown in detail in some of the previous project examples. If you need help, refer back to those step-by-step photos.

To begin, mount all your strands on a clasp (photo 1).

Row 1: Start with the four strands on the very left. Make a square knot, working the two outside strands around the two inside strands. Then move on to the next 4 strands. Again, make a square knot, working these two outside strands around these two inside strands. Continue making square knots across. Lastly make a square knot using the last 4 strands. Photo 2 shows the first row of square knots.

23

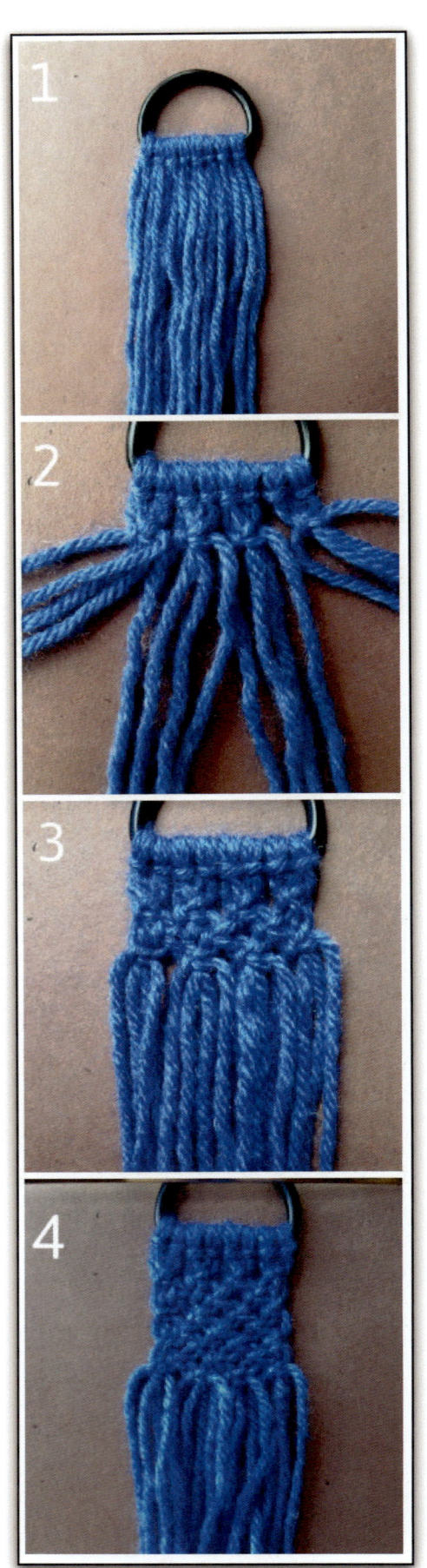

Row 2: For this next row, skip the first 2 strands. Set them aside. With the next 4 strands, make a square knot. Make a square knot with the next 4 and continue across. There will be 2 extra strands at the right-hand edge. Leave these alone. Go on to the next row.

Repeat rows 1 and 2 for your desired length.

Notice how the square knots "alternate" across. You can change the look of your pattern design by making your knots tighter or looser, or leaving more or less space between the rows. Photos 3 and 4 show the progression of the rows.

Josephine knot

This pretty knot can be made with one or two colors. The photos show two colors for ease in teaching the beginner.

Begin by placing your two strands as shown in photo 1. To make this knot, only strand D is "moved" once the initial set up is done. Take D and move it over A, under B, around, over, under, over (as shown in photos 2, 3 and 4).

The knot is completed on step 4 above. All you need to do now is gently tighten (photo 5 below).

To make a second identical Josephine knot, look at photos 6, 7, and 8. Set up your strands as shown in photo 6. Repeat the steps as before, and as in photo 7. Notice how only the orange D strand is "moving."

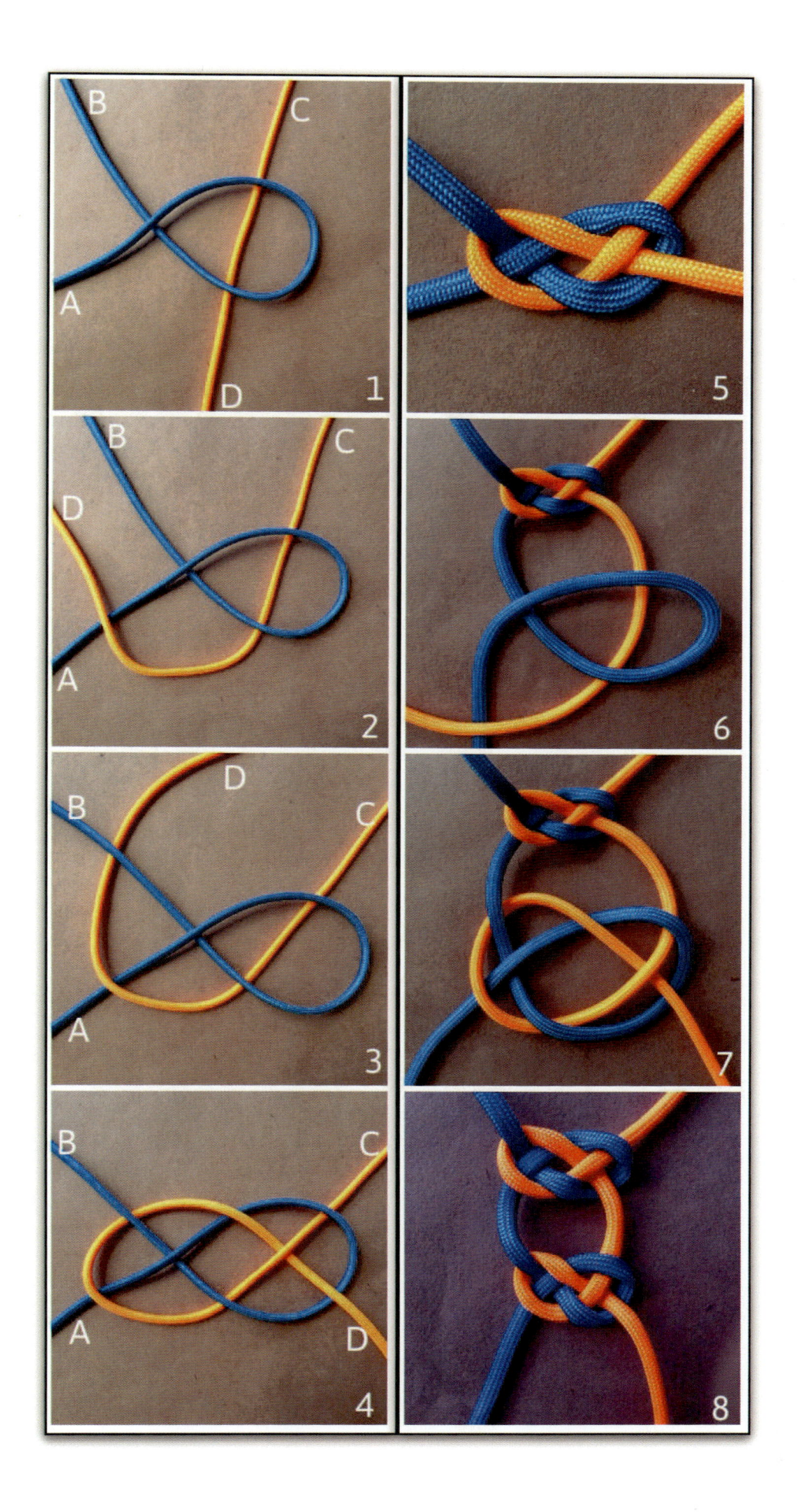

25

Project: Josephine Knot Necklace

To make this necklace, you will need :

- 2 six foot lengths of hemp cord, folded in half for a total of 4 strands. This will make a small necklace of approx. 14" in length. Use longer strands for a longer necklace. (The lengths may vary depending on the spacing of your knots).

- A large bead

To begin, fold your lengths in half and tie an overhand knot to make a loop (photo 1). This loop will need to be just slightly larger than your bead so that the bead will fit through the loop snuggly and won't fall out unintentionally.

Next, set up your strands to make your first Josephine Knot. I have labeled the strands in photo 2 in the same way that they were labeled in the previous example. Remember, once you have the correct set-up, only strand D "moves." You will be working with two strands held together, so this knot will be a little more tricky than working with just one strand. Weave D over-under-over-under-over as shown in photo 3 (remember, more detailed step-by-step photos are in the previous example with the paracord).

Gently tighten your knot as shown in photo 4 and make your next Josephine knot. Continue making Josephine knots, spacing to your liking (photo 5).

To finish, tie an overhand knot, thread a bead, and tie a second overhand knot. Trim the ends and your necklace is complete (photo 6).

27

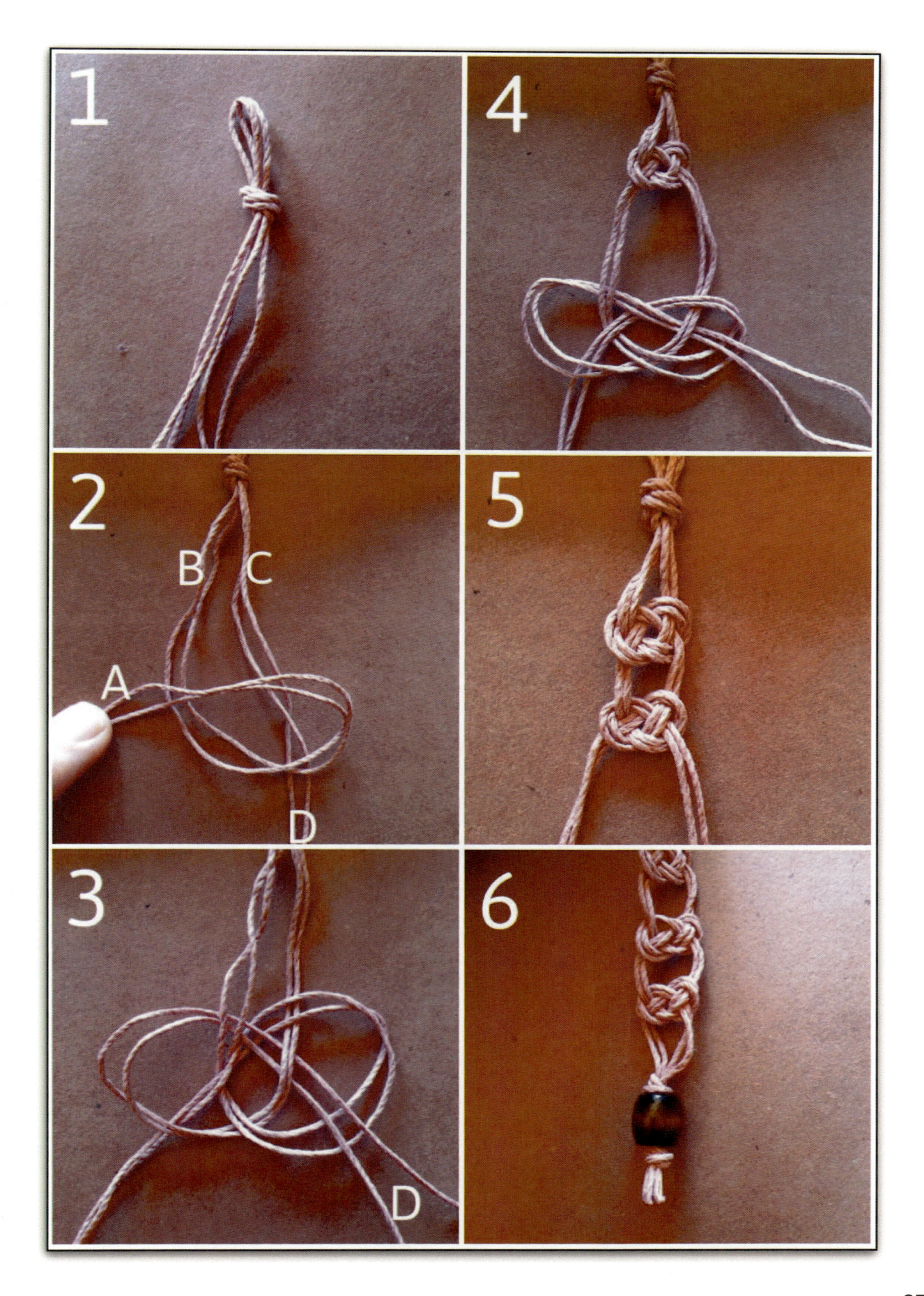

Turk's Head

This knot is very similar to the Josephine knot, but it uses only one strand. In the photos I have intentionally worked it loosely to show a beginner the steps. I have also exaggerated the size of the top loop to show how the bottom part looks just like the Josephine knot.

To begin, start with the set up in photo 1. The length on the left side will need to be about twice as long as the length on the right side. Notice how this set up is pretty much the same as the Josephine knot except that there is a loop at the top. Therefore, I have kept the same A and D labels.

Next, tie the Josephine knot, referring to the photos from the previous section if needed (photo 2).

Now, take your A strand and form a fourth loop on the bottom, bringing it around to match up with the D strand. Your A strand will now follow the path of the D strand (photo 3). Keep following the strand around, matching your A up with it exactly. Follow over and under until you have at last reached back to your D strand (photo 4).

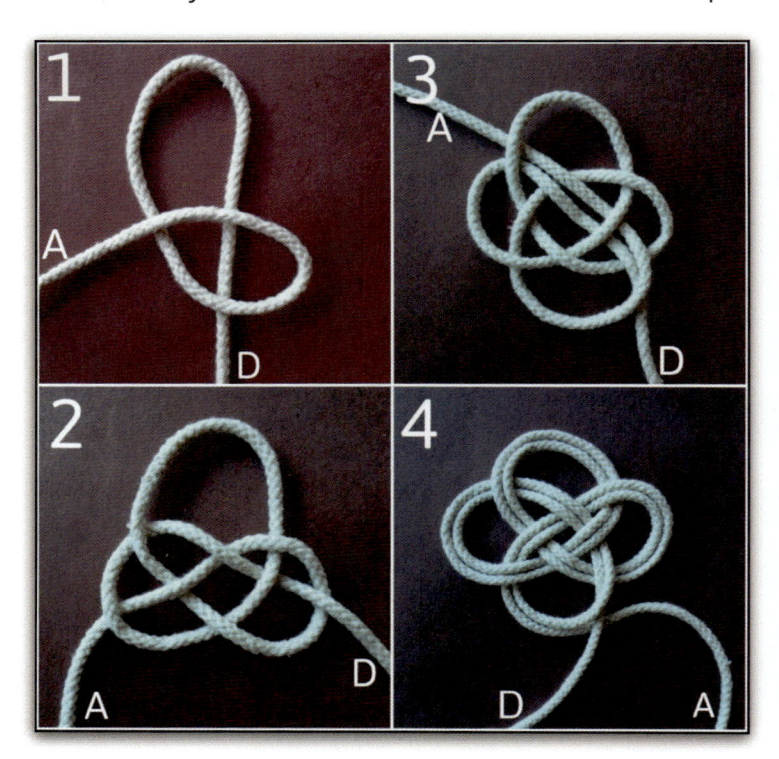

You now have a Turk's Head knot. You can tighten it up so that it looks more like the photo above, or you can keep it loose if you like.

Project: Monkey's Fist

This fun knot is basically an extension of the Turk's Head. Start with one very long piece of cord, about 8 feet or so. Make your Turk's Head as shown in the previous example, but keep continuing your A strand around a third and fourth time. For this project I used a thinner nylon cord, but of course any time of string or rope can be used.

Once you have continued around at least 4 times (see photo below), tighten up your knot. This can take some time and patience. As you tighten, the knot will "fold in" on itself and will turn from flat to a more 3D form. Insert a small ball or marble in the middle of the knot, and continue to tighten until it forms tightly around the ball. And that's it, you have a monkey's fist!

Braiding with Multiple Strands

Braiding is not exactly "knot tying" but it creates pretty patterns that look woven together, so I thought I'd include a little tutorial on how to braid multiple strands. Use an odd number for an evenly laid braid. Let's start with 5 as in the example worked above with blue paracord.

In the photos below I used different colors so you can see how the strands are woven together. First, separate your strands, with 2 on the left and 3 on the right (photo 1).

Take the outside right strand. Weave it under then over so that it can then join the left side group. Now there are 3 strands on the left and 2 on the right (photo 2).

Take the outside left strand. Weave it under then over so that it can join the right side group. Now there are 3 on the right and 2 on the left (photo 3).

Keep taking the outside strand of the group of 3 and weave it under-over to join the other side (photo 4). Repeat this and you get a nice 5 strand braid (photo 5).

Braiding with 7 or More

When using more strands, it is the same basic concept. Start with an odd number of strands and separate into two groups. One group will have an extra strand.

Take the outside strand of largest group, and weave it under/over/under/over etc until you reach the center and it can join the other group.

The photos below show the steps of braiding with 7.

Separate into a group of 3 on the left and a group of 4 on the right (photo 1). Take the outside right strand and weave under-over-under and join it to the left group (photo 2). Take the outside left strand and weave it under-over-under and join it to the right group (photo 3). Take the outside right strand and weave under-over-under and join it to the left group (photo 4). Take the outside left strand and weave it under-over-under and join it to the right group (photo 5). Get the pattern? Continue in this manner, tightening the braid as you go (I left it pretty loose in the photos for explanation purposes), and you will soon have a pretty braid as shown in photo 6.

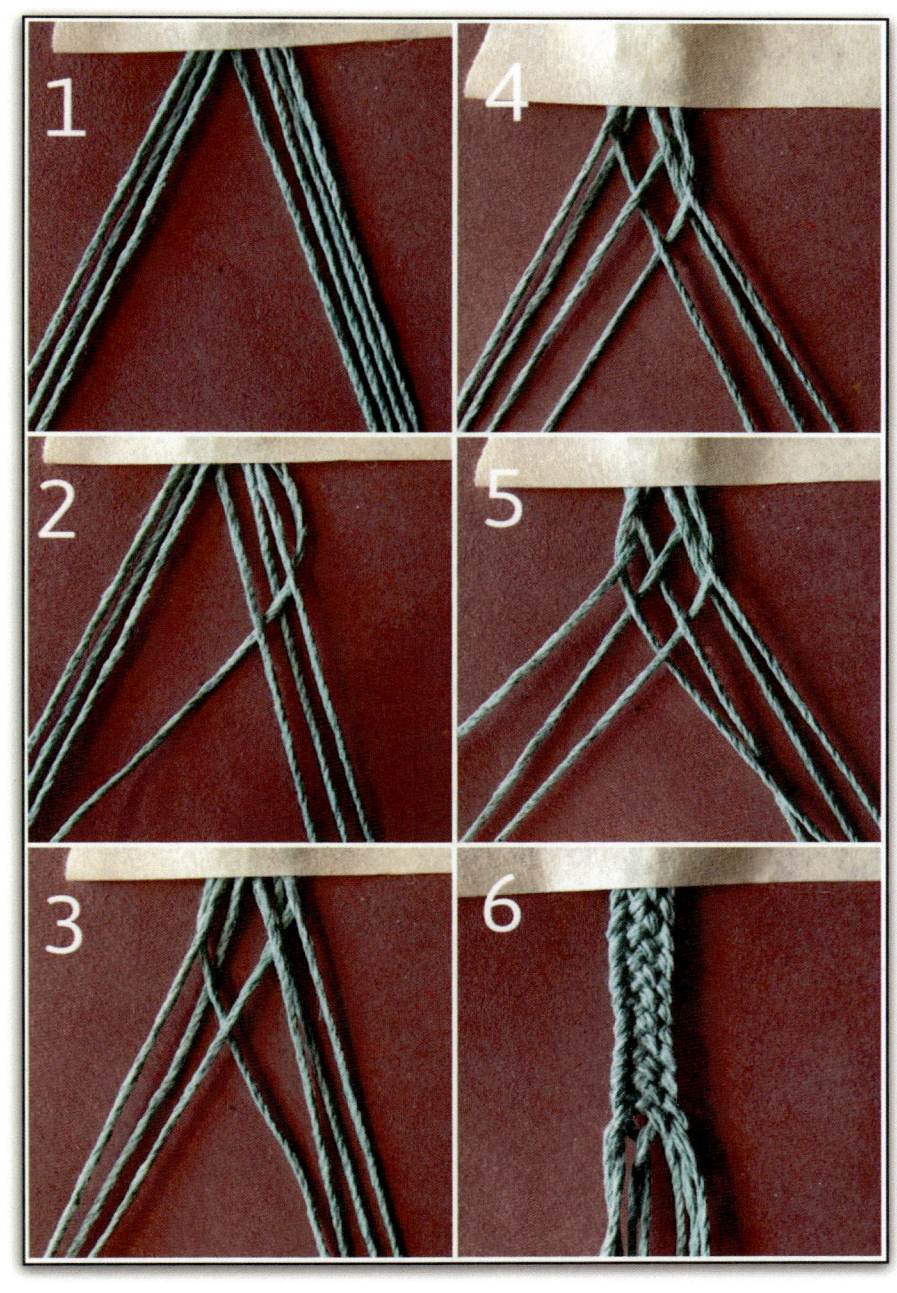

Chinese Crown

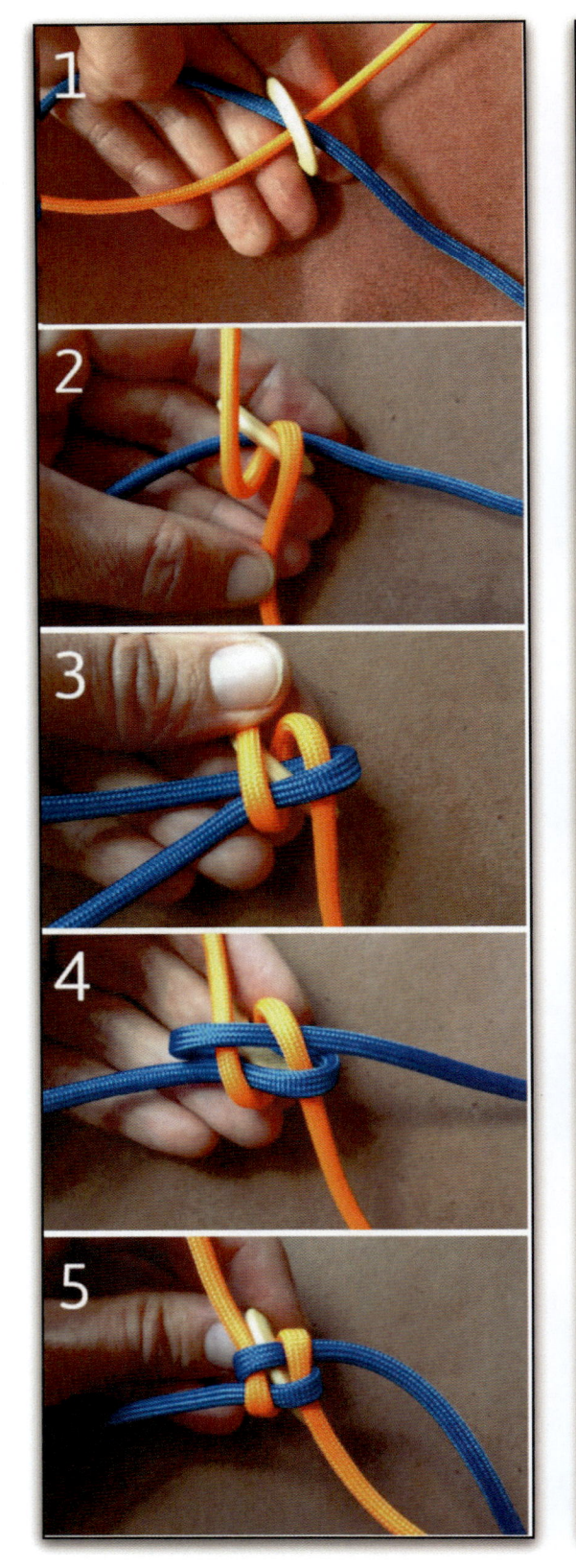

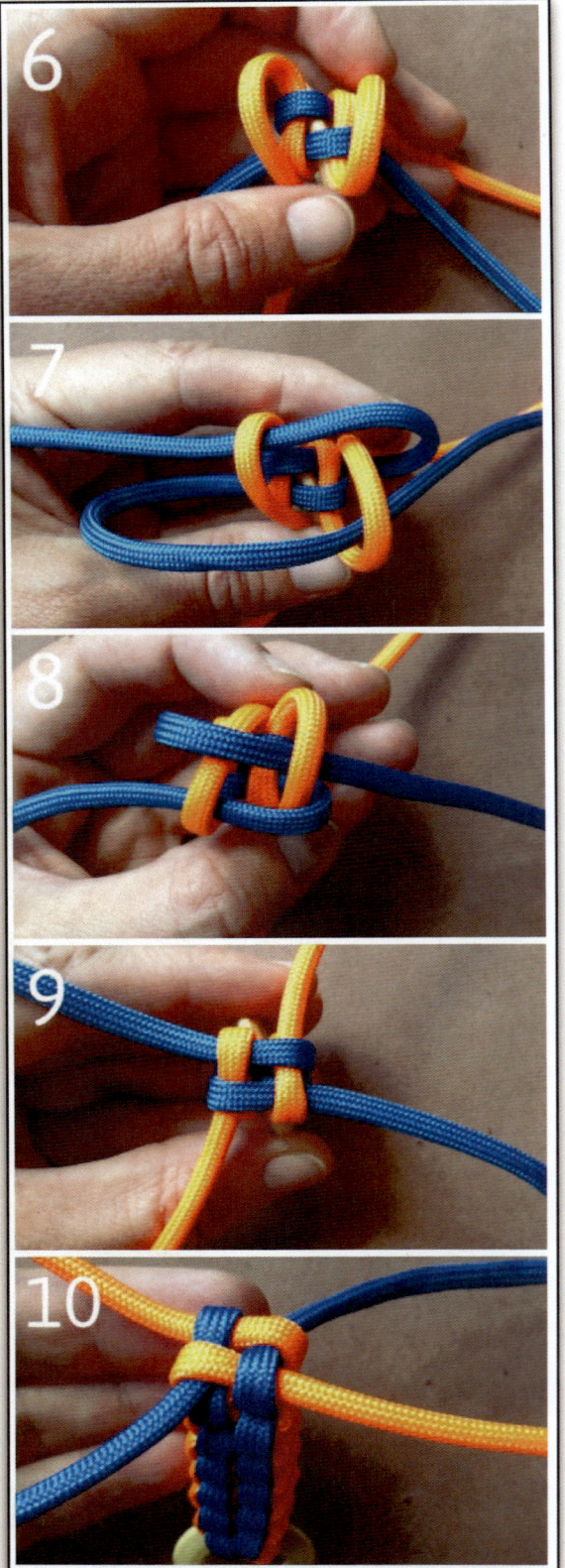

This knot makes an intricate square pattern, but it is not a very difficult knot to make. In fact, when I was a young child we would use plastic lacing and make these at summer camp!

You will need two long strands and a ring/clasp to make the Chinese Crown. I recommend using two different contrasting colors so you can see the pattern better.

To describe how to make this knot, I will refer to the strands as "orange" and "blue" as in the photos.

Start by threading your two strands through the ring in an "X" shape as shown in photo 1. The ring should be in the very center of each strand. The orange should be under the blue.

Take the orange strand and form two vertical loops as shown in photo 2.

You will now take your blue strands and loop them over, weaving them horizontally over-under the orange loops. Photo 3 shows one blue strand worked, and photo 4 shows the other blue strand worked. You now have a nice "square" pattern. Pull all four strands to tighten (photo 5).

The trickiest part about this knot is the beginning. The bottom side will look like an "x" as shown in the photo.

Once you have your first square, the pattern is the same. Fold your orange loops backwards, matching them up vertically again (photo 6). Then take the blues and weave them over-under, matching them up horizontally (photo 7). Tighten into a square (photos 8 and 9). Photo 10 shows the pattern emerging. Just keep repeating the steps in photos 6-9.

Now you have a completed Chinese Crown - repeat to make as long as you would like!

Thanks for Reading and Enjoy!

Tiger Road Pattern Book #010

Tara Cousins

Printed in Great Britain
by Amazon